The Biographical Library of the Old Testament

By

Yvonne Porter Young

All rights reserved

copyright May 2017
Authentic Writings & Photos from internet
Author claims no ownership of photos

The bible stories and their original writings

The contents of versions and chapters written to understanding and comprehend as King James descriptions of authenticates.
Photos are originated from website and are found on internet. The Author is not claiming ownership of any pictures compiled into the book.

True sayings and reservations of authors and experiences, in real life portrait of beginning and end. Insomuch, of how the father, Son, and Holy Spirit created and gave insight of what was, is, and will continue to be.

Yvonne Porter Young

Table of contents
The old Testament

Genesis	*Ecclesiastes*
Exodus	*Songs of Solomon*
Leviticus	*Isaiah*
Numbers	*Jeremiah*
Deuteronomy	*Lamentations*
Joshua	*Ezekiel*
Judges	*Daniel*
Ruth	*Hosea*
1 Samuel	*Joel*
2 Samuel	*Amos*
1 Kings	*Obadiah*
2 Kings	*Jonah*
1 Chronicles	*Micah*
2 chronicles	*Nahum*
Ezra	*Habakkuk*
Nehemiah	*Zephaniah*
Esther	*Haggai*
Job	*Zechariah*
Psalms	*Malachi*
Proverbs	

The Preparation of the Earth
(How the world began)

I am taking this time to share the vision behind a great opportunity of building an interest of inspiration for readers all over the world. Beginning to tell the story, of why I started to preparing learning tools of the Bible, was to inspire others to take part in understanding the word of God. The vision began December, 2016, even though I read the Bible daily over many years, when I began my task of reading a chapter a day as a resolution of faith to the Lord. This was my way of inspiration and connecting with the Lord on a daily communication and prayer time with him. Each day starting with Genesis, Chapter One, January 1, 2017, this is my continuing walk with God and a journey of understanding and realizing how this world truly began.

The inspiration came to me as I continued to read through years pass. I believe we all could use a different direction of vision, with the way the Lord revealed himself in our lives, and how we are able to be the people we are today. Before I continue, I would like to reach out to authors all over the world to address my reason for using the art and beauty of their visions and outstanding graphics of which is seen, and used as part of my project to enhance readers to take an interest in understanding the word of God, and getting to know and applying the vision of God to their lives.

To also note, I take no claims to their outstanding artistry, yet is hopeful in them seeing, where applying the art to the chapters, and learning books of the Bible, helps with bringing alive what truly happened in the stories told. This journey that has inspired me, has been a most astonishing victory of faith of which I hope can be a desire of taking an interest in helping others, to want to take the opportunity to grow in the vision of God, which He daily put before us. The reason behind wanting to share in this way of building a Library of the Old testament with vision, is to help those who do not reconnect with the reading of the original word, can be a learning ability to help them understand the vision and the wondrous works of God.

Starting with the beginning of the Bible, we all know God's master piece of this world began forming in his vision. We know there was darkness. God did something of a great magnificent sight in his vision and began to put his world, which we live in today in preparation for life abundantly.

While reading and understanding how this world was formed and created, the awesome wonder of God's vision, became a vision of faith for me to try and be a part of sharing to others, the preparation of the beauty of which the creation of this world was from by the hand of God.

How do we connect in the inspiration of God's work?

- What would inspire another to take the time to understand the meaning of its preparation?
- How can it be put into perspective for readers to slow down, and really take a look into why God is so important to us as a people of many nations?
- How did we get here?
- Do we know how significant we are?

In writing the stories of the old testament and deciding to take a leap of faith in building a learning tool for others to apply to their understanding and vision, I hope to be able to give to the audience of readers and authors of other inspiring interest, to support each other in growing and being aware of the building in God's wondrous works, and vision of how this world begin. Learning the old testament, the birth of this world, the story of Adam and Eve, Noah, Joshua, and all God's chosen people who were the Israelites. The transformation, throughout the country, as God build his visions through many nations, were a great an inspiring vision of God building His kingdom.

These stories are so inspiring, that as we learn of the preparation of the world. *Does anyone take the time to actually see the total vision of what God did for us to be his people?* Introducing the library as a learning tool of books, broken down to help others to understand the miraculous beauty in God's works, is a leap of faith in teaching others to gradually understand His way. I am still learning God's way, and will always find amazing stories along the way, which keeps me focus on knowing, all I have to do is have the faith the size of a mustard seed, and trust in Him to do His will. I am excited daily to get up every morning and give my time to God, with pray and significant precedence to His word and create what I hope will be prosperous to other.

The Bible stories of which is never told, in some way not addressed in part of a history with kings and saints and nations of nations, as being a life of the beyond. As I read the stories of the old testament and the kings and characters of life, in that time and age, come alive in my readings, the stories give great understanding of how God used them to build, through destructions and the favor to many of which, was so significant to connect in knowing, who and why they existed. From Genesis to Malachi, there is a lot of history behind the amazing stories of which some are not used to apprehend the vision of which God prepared for what comes after into the new beginning of the world, as we know called The New Testament.

My intentions are not for insulting any vision of any one, or demeaning any of the wondrous envisions that are already established. My building a new version of connection with God and sharing my thoughts, creating a vision in the minds of others, as well as a creative thinking, of how God placed before us generations of His signs and wonders, of how he multiplied through the favors of tribes such as the children of Israel, which was chosen by his hand. The stories which will be written, will be inspired for generations, for the glorious and the coming of Jesus Christ his Son, which began in the New Testament Library that will be a part of my learning tools, for the teaching of the salvation of the Father, Son and The Holy Spirit, which stands today.

Creating a vision

The library created by myself starts with children coloring books of the characters, of Genesis, Exodus and continuing through other books of the Bible. The books start with drawings of characters such as, Noah, the Ark, the Tabernacle, the leavened and unleavened bread, Joshua, Pharaoh, Chariots, Moses, Adam, and Eve, and other great characters along with other amazing story histories of which children will come to learn and apply to the knowledge of knowing, who these characters were and how their lives were chosen by God. The perspective of what they character brought to the story of which they lived through the Bible history.

Also, starting with Genesis, I have created the library of learning books to help bring insight to the Bible, for many who may not take interest in knowing where the beginning of time really started. It is true saying, the Lord created heaven and earth and, in the beginning, there was evening. Well, afterwards was what the Lord did to start his vision and gave reality of how the creation of the world came to be. So, the learning technique of My New Version of the Bible is not to change anything, but to use it as a learning technique for those who are interested in wanting to know more of the, Power of God, and why He is a Jealous God, and an Awesome God all in one. We speculate on things of the Bible in such a way that the realism in what is taught to us is not sometimes taken as it should. For example, most of us learn scripture and recite it, because they learn it. Some learn scriptures to say they know the Bible, but yet cannot give true meaning. Then, there is some that are teachers of the Bible, and only uses certain passages to stay focus, and there is some that truly understand from Genesis to Revelations, What God's vision really is.

I'm not an expert far from it, but I do know the more we learn and understand, the more we can believe and apply to our lives, the signs and wonders of what God can do for us. The labeling of ourselves as Teachers, Ministers, Priest, Preachers, Bible experts, Authors and Writers and Readers, are all part of leadership in introducing the wellness of the learning abilities of what was taught to them and to others. My wanting to be a part of sharing history of Bible literature, to the young and old is a great mystery which I would like to unfold, into families, schools, churches, hospitals, and other facilities of faith, and make a difference in some one's life.

These books of learning, which is of great measure of simplifying the Bible is for support for those who would like to make a difference in helping others. My goal is to be a hope of faith for someone, and their love ones, who are struggling with understanding God's word. Believing in His Awesome works, and the most astonishing movement of God, can be a most inspiring grace in knowing, He hear and see everything, also He knows what our destinations are.

As the words say, He knew you before you were born, He knows your future, and knows the desires and needs of which you as a people will experience. He is an awesome God. I hope to establish a connection with this world through the grace of God and with the over powering abilities of knowledge that can be used to build hope and a foundation of which we all can stand on. Also, to be able to testify in truth of what we all experience over time. There are times, we go through things in life and we feel we are alone. Getting to know how God will never leave you, or forsake you, can be of great blessings to you, and believing in these words, can be, because we take out the time to learn more and more of who God is. It is an amazing journey for me. I hope to bring alive in the heart of many, a vision of which will help others to connect with God for their own personal inspiration and interest.

These learning tools of the Library that I have created, will not take the place of the Bible, but can help others to understand and know the Bible in a different perspective. The Bible is a great inspiration and stands strong and mighty in the minds of many throughout the world. There is no competitiveness, or change in God's word, just a building of hope in all we desire to accomplish in His sight, as believers of His miraculous works. To be a part of building a monumental structure of understanding, and most dominating literature of dynamic awesome vision, there is a lot of inspiration and identifying opportunities of what can be a moment of trust in knowing He has not and will not forsake those who believe in Him and in His word. God is powerful and true, and can be the one thing that changes your whole entire world if you continue to believe in Him.

My desire to write and share how I feel the word and miraculous works of God can be a great support and a mentor of hope for you as saints and believers, is a new vision that can be applied daily. Just believing what can be accomplished by learning and achieving what is in our hearts. Sharing with others what is of his creation, and how you were chosen as a people to grow and use Him as a part of your building faith. We grow and sometimes there is a halt in how we grow in faith. Yes, we take to ourselves in many ways and decide we can do, but still the desire of needing God and connecting Him on our daily lives can sometime be pushed aside.

As you read books of faith and be a part of bible studies and workshops of great learning tools, the significant meaning of this is to make it a foundation in your life not just for you, but for love ones, families, friends, congregations of Christ, and the connection of faith around the world. To reach across the world with belief that God can only use a finger to move in miraculous ways the word of which He gave to us in stories and in memorial hope of His son, who went to Calvary for all not just for some, has a most dynamic resort of spiritual inspiration we all share.

The most interesting part of taking an interest in God's word is to help in forming the passion of His magnifying spirit and to give desire of hope to wanting to grasp his spirit and live as His servant. We all come with a purpose. There is a question in everyone's mind. *What is my purpose?* You can only find out if you take the time to understand God's word and apply it to your everyday life and use it as a family balance and personal interest of who you are.

The questions that comes to mind would be:

- Who am I?
- What is my purpose?
- Where do I fit in?
- How can I share God's vision?
- How to teach others to trust that He is God alone?
- How can teaching others to be mindful of how they can be a hope for others?

These simple questions may not mean much to anyone, but they can carry a powerful impact on a person who needs to understand your vision. They would need to know, why you chose to move as God's servant in helping them to understand their purpose.

The vision of God and how the world began

Yvonne Porter Young

In the old testament, God's vision the journey everyone should want to take time in taking an interest as I have, is to get to Know Why, God is who He is. The Old Testament teaches us, the preparation of the earth, the world, and what took place day after day, time after time, and years after years, of transformations, and life of which occurred back in that time of the beginning. In the beginning there was Darkness. God molded something out of darkness and gave light to it. He gave man, stars, moon, and earth. In the passion of God's sight, he did much to build the world, whereas, He seen it before it all took place. Because of His most magnificent design of the world, He also gave an inspiring desire in the minds of his people. As we know reading the Old Testament can be discouraging, because you would think, because God is a passionate and promising God, there was a lot of what went on before this world was able to be formed into a life everlasting.

Taking the time in reading and adjusting the minds around the activities of what had to go on, we all would find out how jealous God really is. If you would look, the design and preparations of life then and now, are not as different as we may think. God had chosen a people in the mix of it all, and brought them out of bondage. As of today, there is still of existence of the Israelites, and others who can tell stories of what truly was in the days of the Old Testament. Now, I am no expert, do not claim to be, wherefore, there are leaders and mentors all over the world, that have seen and heard and have lived some of what we may wish to understand.

Therefore, my suggestion to any one is to take out time and read word for word the astonishing stories of what God vision and how it is a reality of what we live. If there was not a beginning, we would not exist, therefore taking an interest in why there is still wars of wars, rumors of wars in the old country. Why there will always be rumors of wars. This has been from the beginning of time, starting with Pharaoh, and his army, how he was the king of a great army and was the slave driver over Egypt. Taking the time to recognize *the Canaanites, Hittites, Amorites, Perizzites, Hivites, and the Jebusites and others,* began to read and study the Old Testament, as it is written with the study guides of which I have created along with other spiritual readings.

- Do you know who they were, and why they were significant in the sight of God?
- What about the chosen people of God, and how they were freed of Pharaoh?

In the days of God's preparation, there was a lot of *misfortunes, misunderstandings, rudeness, rebellion, sadness, along with life and death.* God used His people in some horrific ways, to build a world for His son to be born. There were women of strength also, such as Sarah, Zipporah and Rebekah. Israel was the chosen people that God found favor, so He covet them through a journey, which brought them out of Bondage and into a promise land. Even though He continued to give, they rebelled, questioned, and doubted His gratefulness. He never stops carrying them through. God's word was His undying love and His bond of keeping Israel as His chosen people. The Old Testament teaches us preparation in our lives for the next encounter of which we would have to face. Character of who we are and how we can adjust to the comings of what lies ahead.

Though in life, we fall short of our comings, some of the times, is because we are not focus on what we see before us. Then again, it could be, God is put aside for us to take control of what we face, therefore, we fall. God, in the Old Testament, teaches us through the life of many people, and tribes of life, the wages of sin, the downfalls of life, the doubt that is held in the minds and hearts, the failures of life and the amazing rising of life. We did not get here by ourselves, we got here through a whole lot of *vision, ancestry, building, difficulties, depressions, oppressions, emptiness, desires, journeys, and more* of which took place in the days of the Old Testament, through our ancestral life, which is not recognized in some fashion.

There was a lot of nations created through the eyes of God and His hand of greatness, that is a momentum of what He shared to build a world such as this one. There was a time, when God took a great man, all who we know as Moses, to lead His people out of Egypt. There was a lot that had to be done, in order for them to believe God loved them just that much. Moses was His chosen, to lead them out of bondage, therefore, recognize the vision of which is a remembrance. Throughout the Old testament even after *Noah, Moses, Aaron, Joseph, Joshua, Jacob, Isaac, Abraham*, and others. They were great men in the sight of God.

The children of Israel, was the chosen people to be carried through every trial of which God put before them. The *rebellion, fear, and doubt,* was still there in the

Israelites of what God vision was for them. The sacrifices and the building of the altar. Reading and taking an interest in knowing the preparation of this world did not start with fear, it started with *ambition, courage, strength, wisdom, understanding, and knowledge*. Many people came through the experiences of Gods wrath, and His power of mercy. He spoke to His chosen ones; He gave them journeys of which sometimes wasn't so great, but He kept them in the midst.

The promise land,

- Where was the promise land?
- Why was it the place to be?
- Did anyone take the time to understand the vision of which God put before the children of Israel?

There was a lot of bloodshed and mourning, adjusting to what had to be done to get through. The Israelites experienced a lot of authority over them throughout the journeys of their lives. *Tribes of warriors, sacrifices, death,* understanding their ways and why they were chosen. Many questions, and rebellion went through the life of the children of Israel. The Lord told them they would go to a place flowing with milk and honey. There was a lot that had to be, because nothing in life is free, this is what we as a people should know. Along the way, there is many trials that has to pass through, many failures that has to be experienced in order to grow or mature from what we fail from. The Old Testament teaches us about the failures and doubt, fears, grievances and other uncomforting misfortunes of growth.

Yes, growth, because we will always find a reason to question why things always falling apart, soon as we get on track with having a path clear. The reason behind failure is faith in saying to yourself, *this is not where I give up, this is where I began.* To begin to understand you, you have to understand your purpose and apply it to yourself, and knowing the accomplishment in achieving is to not fall, just because of a disappointment, or decision that did not go your way. This is what the children of Israel had to learn, how to believe and not doubt, even though they continue to question God's decisions, they were not left. He showed them punishment, mercy and yes, He was angered by what they would choose to do. Through it all, He kept them, and they were throughout the history of the Old testament, the ones who through generations, can give testimony of what God did for them.

In the Old Testament, God continued his vision by sharing His designs through signs and wonders, how he began with Adam and Eve, man and woman to create in the minds of the interested reader, the way life began after the serpent came to Eve, on the given day to deceive the works of the Lord. To better spin this, Adam was a man which God vision in his own image, to labor the land and watch over it, but in the midst of it all, Adam needed a helpmeet, therefore, God put Adam in a deep sleep and formed from the rib, a woman who is called Eve. They were naked and did not know wrong or right, bad or good. God was pleased at what he had created. At that time, they knew nothing except they were man and woman. He gave them command, for they could eat off any tree, but the one in the midst of the garden. Unfortunately, Eve was under the tree of life, which she was told never to take from. There came a serpent, we all know who this is, and manipulated Eve, putting thought in her head, it would be okay to eat from the tree. Long story short she did take from the tree a fruit. She then went to Adam and told him to take a bite of the apple, which he did.

The story of Adam and Eve, we all should know, is how good, bad, wrong and right became the existence in life changes. God was angered at the awareness that they both was enlightened to acknowledge. They began to see themselves in true light of who they were, knowing they were naked and needed to re-adjust themselves. These stories of adventurous interest are sharing with us the reality of God's vision and the creative awareness of his works, even though the anger and deceit of which the serpent tried to derail. God's power of which he reveals to us comes through the vision of which is still a realistic value even today. As the stories continue to connect through ancestral trait, the story not only shared the forgiveness of God, also the compassion of him.

Then came along the sons of Adam and eve, Cain and Able, which we know the story how Cain was jealous of Able and killed him. Cain then moved away from the Lord and he took a wife, and bared a son E'-noch, he named a city after him. There life began for many of which is unknown to us in this day. God still as he does us in trials times, keep us as he did Cain even though he took the life of his brother, because of zeal, greed, anger and jealousy, we know the story and how God saw through the struggles yet still Cain was blessed to have a son. In other words, God never leave us or forsakes us. Even though this happened, Cain was still blessed.

Moving on to Noah, the next stage of the vision of God, the fact God chose him to build an ark, not just to build it, but to carry in pairs everything that had life. God preparation went beyond the stories told, He had a reason of which we need to take time to acknowledge. He was not only creating a world, He was building something. The creation and the passion of God builds a picture of beauty, fascinating promise, most amazing sight of dynamic stabilities of which we will never be able to imagine. Until these stories can be of reality, there will still be thoughts of why, when, where, and how.

To in vision the power of God and what was going through Him, when He decided to create a world, was an unknown miracle of why we are the people could be of this world today. The Old Testament teaches how God's hand of mercy, hold the key to every turn in our lives. The moon, stars, rivers, land, day, night, hills, valleys, mountains, and the entire beauty of the universe. All of this would not have been, if it wasn't for the Lord, and His creative passion for the world and its growth. In the Old Testament, there are stories that led up to the coming of our Lord Jesus Christ. Wherefore, it all began one day, which was through His father, our Lord God, as he formed man and woman, and day and night. The earth and all that it holds. During the preparation of this world, there were many lives, saints, leaders, followers, families of things we experience today, just back then was not of technology of which we use today.

The Old Testament was about, what should be related to life today. No, we did not exist then, but God knew you would exist in this day. Through the books of the Old Testament, learning how, *Adam, Eve, Moses, Noah, Joshua, Abraham, Isaac and Jacob, Joseph, Isaiah, Samuel, David, Jonathan,* and others were leaders and mentors of their tribes and people, the existence of their names of memories are instilled as a history of which we all should want to share with our children, and the things they had to endure to accomplish their goals. The ten commandments and how they became to commandments of which we are supposed to honor and obey.

After the building of the ark and the Lord told Noah to board two of each life, male and female, this was a vision of which God had for the multiplications of generations. Through preparation, there is much transformation which went on before the time of Pharaoh. As the waters grew and the flood of the earth began the ark that Noah built through the command of God was filled as He wanted. For a while Noah, his family and all the life of which was on the ark, was there until life of one root. This life was showing that the earth was ready for the beginning of a transformation, where everything on the ark was able to be let out and to rome the earth. It all started with a dove, which Noah sent out to look over the land to find life, but there was none to be found. What the dove found was an olive leaf which he plucked.

Noah then knew it was time to release all the animals and the fowls of the air. There was a nation descended from Noah, generations of generations. The great stories that followed Noah and the generations that were of great force, came to pass. Noah aged and everything of God's creation was of great purpose. The fascinating vision of God and the inspiring stories began to be passionately created through the power of God. Then there was the building of the great temple, where the altar of the Lord was a daily offering of sacrifices. When Moses became the leader of the children of Israel, they were taken from bondage of Pharaoh. In the story of Israel, they confirmed the covenant, the Ark of the testimony. This was a great memorial of the great temple, which was through the journey of the children of Israel. We all know the story of the bondage of the children of Israel, and how they were witnesses of what powers God had to bring them out of the bondage of the Egyptians.

The Old Testament teaches of the offerings and the commandments of God, and what went on with the leavened and unleavened bread, the bullock, the sacrifices of which they had to bring before God, peace offerings. The burnt offerings, sin offerings, and how they were a way of forgiveness in the sight of God. The truth of what life, was in those days will to come to pass in the days of beyond. There were moral laws, laws of redemption, laws concerning slavery. The history behind the history is a fascinating design of which God has prepared us to see, only if we can believe in his miracles of truth. When Moses was above all, God told him to go to the mount Si'-nai, where he revealed himself to Moses. He was told to demand the census of the Israelites and to number them by generations. Through it all there were tribes of thousands. These were very big tribes of which grew over time. Many things were going on in this time.

There was a special tribe of which the Lord excused the Levites whom were not to be touched. As Moses and God communed in the mountain of Si'-nai, the children of Israel complained and acted out and even made an image of a calf and worshipped it. We all know what that story did. The anger of God and the powerful wrath that was witnessed by the children of Israel. Moses was told by God to go and adjust the situation. He did and he threw the tablets of stone down on the people and shewed the anger of which they have brought. Moses was chosen by God to lead the people out of bondage and into the promise land.

God work was hard, but He never gave up on the children of Israel. They were still his chosen people. To get better understanding, I advise you to pick up your Bible and read the stories told to better bring knowledge to you, of what went on in the days of the Old Testament, and how we got to this place in our lives. Throughout the stories, God's anger for the Israelites were not to leave them, but to continue to use them as witnesses to what He can do. Not only then but now. Moses, through all God's glory, was to make sure the Ten Commandments were written and used through all generations of life. There were so many ways of realizing God is still in control, to the amazing transformations of how each time a powerful chosen person was by the hand of God. The stories elevated and began to connect in the time of Moses and the time of Joshua. There is much to learn about the Bible stories and how they connect with us as a people. There are many learning strategies from authors all over the world, inspiring people to take the opportunity to learn and understand, the many ways God's great inspiration, signs and wonders of his miraculous works all began.

The finding of your own vision, is up to you as a person of purpose and wanting to know what your purpose is, and how you apply it. The books that I have designed are learning books to understand the stories in a different way and to help many that come in your path, the most astonishing desires of God's compassion. The stories told were of great knowledge and strong faith in what was witnessed by the people who were able to leave with us, legacies of true living momentums of people who came through the time of the great transformation of this world to the day of our God's Son Jesus Christ. Before Jesus the Son of God, there was much more to explore and to understand. Through my reading and writings, I will give my thoughts of how the Old Testament is the first sight of the world and its ruins. The *mountains that stood, the valleys that flowed, the rivers that traveled miles and miles,* and how this world is God's world and everything that is a part of it, *man, beast, fowls of the air, and everything crawling on the earth, and every creature which swims in the seas.*

The need of connecting is also a way of knowing what your purpose is. I will continue to asked you to pick up the Bible, read and focus what each story brings to the transformation of this world and how God has all power. He also is the creator and the leader of you. Take learning tools of other readings, such as my learning tools, and of other authors and research and find the true meaning of how the world and God's vision interact with us as a people today.

Throughout the Bible there are great and strong force that is among the people of which God used to prepare his great nation of this day. All the while his desire and design for us, I would say, is to know the good and bad of each part of our comings and goings, and decisions we make as a people. God's power is greater than anything we have designed this universe with. My hope is, that we as a people will know every tool, every ground, every city, country, nation, and individual will always recognize all this came from the mind and expertise of decision making and planning. The structures of buildings, the making of cities and the strength of the mind and labor of all. God placed everything before us as a tool to build nations of nations, from generations to generations.

Technology is a part of the designs of minds and creativity to design and structure the industries of today. This was still some of what was back in the history of the Old Testament. The creativity of the beginning, *the great stones of the Ten Commandments, the tools to build the Tabernacle, the ark of the covenant, the Noah's ark, the Ephod and the Breastplate, the candlestick, and other magnificent things* God placed before them, and us. The Old Testament teaches us how to prepare for what comes next in our lives. In those days things was a bit different, but yet the same, because we all have decisions of how we live our lives, *how we raise our children, how we make part in building the kingdom, or cities of which we live, how we are still nations of nations, and generations of generations,* who need to be reminded of who they are and how they get to be at this point in their lives. Making a difference, continue to believe in God and his power, sharing the connections through testimonial blessings.

We do not live alone, even though sometimes we feel we are alone.

God is always looking down on us,

- He is always in our lives.
- He silent, but yet moves when we stand still,
- He brings peace just at the moment of triumph,
- He shares his passion when our hearts are broken,
- He is the magician at the time of disaster,
- He is the shadow that follows every whim of our lives.
- How do we describe the beauty of God?

Look around at the world and the things He put before us to use as tools to build *shelters, medical industries, homes, financial institutions, educational institutions, roads traveling in and out and all around.* There is much to learn about the vision of which God have seen over generations of life. Using the Bible and the tools through authors and their experiences and in-cites on what they have presented over centuries of research and witnessing the inspiring stories told, can be a true inspiration of encouragement to wanting to study more.

In the Old Testament we learn the books of the bible, which is better known as a journey of courageous kings, leaders and chosen people, whom God himself gave vision to. All of what we read is written in the Books of Chronicles in such a way of bringing understanding to each reader and audience of faith. By engaging in the knowledge of how God's vision, also, how He prepared all that is here today through the hands of many nations, the sacrifices of which he shows us throughout the journey, carries an amazing focus of which we all can envision.

Perhaps, not for some, however, for those who have faith and believe that God can do all things but fail, shares a powerful message which is taught generation to generation. As I continue my journey of getting to know God and his powerful works, the message of hope is a gift of which we can share among all people. Learning, leaping, applying abundantly the purpose of knowing God is the greatest gift we as a people can share through our own journeys of experiences, trial, tabulations, sacrifices, failures, strengths, blindness, vision, desires also salvation. We as a union of nations has come full circle of many bruises, however the bruised of which God used for the life of which we live, was sacrifices of which He used to build a universe of greatness, through His own powerful hand of grace and mercy.

The preparation as I have said, of the Old Testament was for His son, and all He applied to his being. The option of wanting or needing to know the most powerful God is really up to you as an individual. The knowledge of how you can be a blessing to someone, is having faith, and acknowledging God as your Lord and savior, knowing His son went to Calvary for you and I. knowing what He did for us, is a start in wanting to know about His vision of preparation for His son **Jesus Christ**, who came and rescued you from many obstacles which stand before us each day.

I am not claiming to be a perfect piece of this journey; however, I am learning the power of God and all He has done. Also, knowing He will not forsake you or leave you. As the words of the Lord stand, "If my people, which are called by my name, shall humble themselves, seek my face, turn from their wicked ways, then will hear from heaven their sin, and will heal their land." How we need the Lord, how we bow down, how we accomplish anything, has to come through trusting the sufficiency of his word. By His grace and Mercy, the abundance of His power is in us. Putting on the whole Armor of God is showing Him we believe in His word, knowing all things are possible through Him.

I ask once again;

- Can you do it on your own?
- How can you find peace in life without God?
- What steps would you take to receive abundance?
- Will you be willing to save a life by the experiences of your own?
- Will you use the word of God to be a pathway for the loss?

Finding time to read and apply the word of God for the revealing of his works, can be a prosperous levitation of growth. Believing in self and helping someone through to save a soul is a part of our purpose. Praises go up, blessings come down, how do we know this. For some, searching is reading the word of God and applying to you and others. The more we learn, the more we teach, the more we build in God's kingdom, the more He give us. Our young, needs to know they can count on us to leave them with the support of God's promise and know this is where they can go to get the answers they need when we are no longer available. I hope all of us know we are not here forever, just for a little while.

Sharing with others, is a significance of helping the generation coming after us, now lay your treasures in heaven where moth or dust cannot corrupt, where thieves cannot break in nor still. I know I am an amateur of psychology, but I do know God has all power and He control our lives, even thou we do what we want, only to fall. Know God allow things to be so, in other words, He do not stop you, He waits and covets you through anything you go through. We need to make changes for the generation coming in, to prepare for a journey of which all of us will go. My mother said when she knew her time of going home, "Ask now for anything you need from me, because where I'm going there is no phone to call." My uncle said, "I will be at my new address right on the inside of the gates, where I will be singing in the choir up yonder."

When reading the word of God in each story, there is a significant tell of how the chosen leaders and all who was commanded and used in moving forward in the vision of God, is a lesson in learning how powerful He is. The searching of purpose of which we all find ourselves doing, is written. Finding your purpose in sharing with others, the greatness in changes occurring in us continually. The focus of how chosen people of God's power were rulers, leaders, priest, warriors, brave men and women, who gave their loyalty as faith, whereas, some refused. Take time to understand His preparation for His Son. There was much confusion, and sadness in the days of old. God's power was so great the belief in knowing his hand sifted and molded this world, whereas, man has built the grounds to their own desires and trends, which we live, and endure. However, God put the tools before us, we used them to the advantages of which we choose. The world itself is still of God's greatness, which we have saturated it with many visions beyond the boundaries of our habitations. So much has conspired over generations, whereas, we as a people forget who is in charge.

- What are our purposes in life?
- Who are we to judge?
- How is it we can be descendants and not be accountable for who, or what we have become?
- Can we find our purpose?
- Can we go backward, is there a possibility in change?
- Do we teach His Gospel, Sing His praise, Pray His prayer, and still fall short of the glory of the Lord?

Just questions we may have already thought of, and learned from. Then again, maybe not, because of society and where it is headed. The stories haven't changed much, we as a people, has overlaid, and overlaid, one thing after another, because of the many desires before us. The Bible and the chain of events, has not been a faultier, it has been an inspiring factor in life history. God's preparation and His plan will always be, because He will always be God all by Himself. The Bible is a very powerful and significant part of society's growth, even though many do not read or care to know God's preparation and His purpose.

Understand the changes and the significant values of what is ahead for this world. Whether man feel he can reach the ultimate high, God still has the power to tear it away. It is so important for us as a people of faith and great intuitions and vision, to understand nothing we do can ever reach the power of God and what He will do. Reading the Bible and the entirety of it helps the understanding of how it is, also it will always be a part of our society growth. Man takes and shifts it around, God still see what man is capable of, He knows our every move, thought, dreams, desires, and our actions. God sees and hears every word and activity we are creating in this society. The trends of what man is doing, and the desires of which we as humans create in our minds. Believe me not when I say, God is watching and the world is in a birthing motion of being shifted and no one can understand the loss and disasters of why.

In the stories told from Genesis to Malachi, generations of generations, have come and gone. As we continue to justify the works of God, we find there are some things which we are still trying to take a grip to know, how He did it all. No one really know God except God. His majestic power and grace, which humbles us through each story. Reading and sharing in a different formation, is not telling you I am changing anything of his works, I find in inspirational and inspiring to just revealing Him in a light of passion as of who He is. The might God of power, the Magnificent measure of grace, the Armor of Righteousness, Salvation, Glory and Truth. These stories, should be a need of restoration for many, because of how you grow in His vision, and feel with the compassion in His powerful hand. God is in all we do, good and bad. He knows you, He made you, He knows your heart, mind and soul. The being of you, belongs to Him. My Pastor, of The Church Without Walls, once said, "We are the dust of the earth," and he is so right. There are so many scripture readings that is quoted throughout the bible, therefore I will not quote. I believe all things do work through our God, and also for the good. He is the creator, and the mediator of our lives. I am really enjoying my journey. I do believe God is and will always be.

- When do you believe?

- What do you believe?
- How do you believe?
- Can you believe in the majestic wonders of God's Will?

My life change is so inspiring to me, because I have nothing to prove to no one, I am so free willed to know God is my God, and I know He will not fail me. I can only fail myself. In other words, don't blame Him for being who He is. We are going to lose along the way to His glory, because that is how He work. Pay attention to the stories, you will see, the hand of God, and how the tools He uses is already in place. You are a part of His creation, also you are used as a part of his works.

As the journey unfolds parts of our live through the destress of being who we are, the Bible teaches us the disciplinary statutes of how God as our intercessor, carries us through the fundamentals of our experiences of faith. Through the stories told the maturity of faith, hope and prosperity, comes from what the teacher teaches us through His life challenges of knowledge, which we all as His people lack in grabbing hold of His power, above all power. Even though each book has its own dynamic revelation of the majestic works of God, they also give us a revealing photographic insight to the journey of which continues in life today. God and the power of which we consume in our lives, helps us to know His Truth, Salvation, His Righteousness, His shield in Grace and Mercy, for there is none like Him.

We all know He is the Father, the Son and the Holy Spirit. We also know He is the creator of all things. We also know He fights all our battles. God is majestic and is great in all He do. The sincerity of His journey, teaches us of how the saints, leaders and chosen ones, came to be of a historical monumental foundation in the life of which we have. Taking for granted the word of God and all of which He does, can be a falling short of his glory, for not believing his word. We all know his word is sufficient in every way.

Through each book, God shows His hand of Mercy, Grace, and Wonderous works continually through his people, through leaders chosen by His hand of whom were with transgressions as well as iniquities. Often, we find ourselves wrestling with ourselves, in the things we take on to do ourselves, and we somehow find, mind you, we cannot do anything without the hand of God.

- Believing
- Trusting
- Rejoicing
- Consuming

Knowing His Grace and Mercy is sufficient, we as His people, generation to generation, nations to nations, all have to understanding the righteousness of God.

To consume the entirety of what is written for us as a people, the children of God, we have to embrace in Him, the trust of His power.

In the books of which is individually being created, there is a journey of which we all need to be empowered by. God's true identity with us. Yes, we fall short each day in one way or another, however, we learn by bowing down and asking for restoration in Grace, He is the God of the creation. In the books of Psalms where I have been for a few months, I notice the majestic power of how we are witnesses of what David and others prayed for, praised for and believed in. In the book of Psalms, finding,

- Grace
- Mercy
- Deliverance
- Power

There are so much of which is consumed in the hearts and mind of all of us to understand the power of which God works.

- Trust
- Faith
- Joy
- Praise

David in Psalm prays for deliverance, relief from torment, for wisdom, for blessings, forgiveness, salvation, revelation, and other wonderous works of which God hands of mercy was revealed.

Through the prayers as I meditated on what is written, there were times the revealing powers of God's wonderous works, was a witness of what He can do through my own family experiences. Not only that, but through the storms that came our way, there were miracles after miracles of what God do. There are other names in Psalms who gave recognition to the wonderous of God;

- Chief Musician
- Maschil, for the sons of Korah
- Shoshannim, for the sons of Korah
- A Psalm of Asaph

There were so many who was mention in the book of Psalm such as;

- Shushaneduth
- Aramnaharaim
- Aramzobah
- Joab
- Neginah
- Jeduthun

As you can see my books are not quite as direct as the Bible, but is created individually and is written as such. The design of these books is to help those who may need support in learning the Bible in a different form of achievement. Therefore, my vision and journey are supported by the hand of God, in form of helping others to understand the ways, also, to know the preparation of God's vision, is of His own through authors and of ancient witnesses of knowing what took place in the history of time.

In the book of Psalm, the identifying the names of Asaph, and of the sons of David, are recognized such as in Book III,

- Maschil of Asaph
- Altaschith, son of Asaph
- Neginoth, son of Asaph

- shoshannimEduth Psalm of Asaph
- Gittith Psalm of Asaph

There are others saints who was sharing their Psalm of prayers through the Book as did David;

- Aleph, Beth, Gimel, He, Daleth, Vau, Zain
- Cheth, Teth, Jod, Caph, Lamed, Mem, Num
- Samech, Ain, Pe, Tzaddi, Resh, Schin, Tau

Who would you say they were and how would you describe their positions as saints of the Psalms?

We truly need to take the time to learn and remember as we read to understand why God's Grace and Mercy is upon us as His children, from generations pass, to generations now, and to the generation of our future ancestry of which will be as long as God is in control and can continue the preparations of this world.

There are decrees of Solomon and of David, which was shared through the historical vision of God and the power of song. The saying, "Sow in Tears, Reap in Joy," the decrees of which was prayers for the righteous of God, the exception of God, the depth of crying for the Lord, the hope in the Lord, the remembrance in the Lord, the abundance, also, the blessing of the Lord.

In the Book of Psalm, we learn the endurance of the Lord's Mercy, we know it is forever, this is why we give thanks and know He is God.

Through the Book of Psalm, we also learn the perfection of knowledge and how we need God to search us, through our hearts, minds, and souls, for the deliverance of the things we create in our own minds, as well as our hearts and souls. We always will need God to undo or to grab hold of us with His unchanging hands of Mercy. We are our own enemies; we take for granted what He has given to us and we destroy the goodness of it because of who we are.

In God we are kept, by His grace and Mercy we are kept, through prayer we are kept, through his majestic works we are kept. The Lord is praised through all trials and of all tribulations. How majestic is his name? The vision of God is our lives and we need to know the journey of faith and hope is of what we believe and how we apply it to our lives.

Creating this biographical piece, is a difficult one and hope the vision of it can reach others to bare forth the hope to not only give, but to also receive the Grace of which God can share as a whole on everything we do.

The book of Proverbs, fascinating and powerful, the inspiring method of wisdom and how it is the center of what life can throw at you. We deal with difficulties in our lives daily. Most of the time we are trying to fix our own situations, however, if we learn wisdom and how to be still, and know there is a God, we can use our mental and physical activities of growth to understand the path of which God has already laid out for us. Getting acquainted with the excellence of wisdom and knowing how powerful it can be, is a significant ability in righteousness, and the deliverance of what we endure as a people.

Proverbs teaches us value,

- Guidance,
- Merit,
- Awareness

- Wisdom and honor.

The readings can be astonishing to share and reveal the orders of God steps in the sight of our own creative attractions. It also tells of man, the creativities and pleasures of how he can be wicked, and righteous equally.

During the journey of Proverbs, it speaks of man and woman, wherefore, a righteous man speaks truth, a strong woman builds her house. Proverbs helps us to understand things of the heart, and the mischiefs of fools. Also, Proverbs teaches us knowledge, knowledge of failure and how to stand in the midst of a storm. The creativity of which we all fall into periodically relates to what is taught by the word of God, of how we should fear God and know He is God. Wisdom and the meaning behind it, is a multiple value of richness for man.

Knowing the confidence built by God in man and the deliverance of which we receive from Him, is shared in the reading of Proverbs. God is only saying be still for I Am God, the creator and the messenger of all things. This journey is a lesson of many magnificent forces of which has help me through many storms. If you read to study and apply what God is teaching us as His people, we can overcome the darkness that always and follows in sorrow and in difficult times. Trusting God and knowing Him through Proverbs can mature the soul and mind of us all. Miraculously, God has all power and shares with us the strength behind knowledge and truth.

The confidence in self is a product of faith, and the hand of God to know He can carry us through any trial and error we deal with in our lives. Being persistence and eager to move forward and not fall through our hardship, is taking the initiative to bring forth the reality of life and deal with our situations with the hand of God.

In daily life, we have challenges of which we create ourselves. Yet in the midst, we forget the significance of the will, in which God instills in us. There are many episodes in our lives where we have taken control and have destroyed our own desires and thoughts, because of self-control of what we prefer built alone. Leaving God out of the equation, can only show disaster, or better word failure in the plans we make. God's plan shares a more defined structure for us to envision in His sight. This world has transformed in many levels, designs, also, structures of idols of which many praises. God's plan for us is not a light weight of decision, it is the decision of which He will make.

We live in a society of temporary fix, which is made up of;

- Desires   Visions   Predictions
- Creativities   Ownerships and more,

This world was design by one vision and one preparation of the hand of God. The preparation was for His Son who was bruised for our transgressions, our iniquities, and for our lives, which He already knew were going to be of, rebellion, abuse, cursed, failures, richness, success, abstinence, destruction, denial, lying, cheating, abomination, false worshipping, prayer, stumbling, sacrificing, the list continues. However, this is not something that we as a people seem to take strongly. Taking the time to read and experience the word of God, shares the compassion of his power, knowing the sides of both anger and compassion, there is a God of which we should fear. As we develop a part of us, which we never interceded with, we find more of who we are.

We learn how selfish we are, how compassionate we are, how defined we are, the depth of what we do in order to succeed. Whereas, God has the right to take it away at any time. Can we be honest with self, to know nothing is hidden from the sight of God, the higher power above all things? There is so much to learn, for we are still naïve to what is reality. Everything is of ruins, if God desires to take it from you. In the times we live in today, there is so much that is being allowed, because of the coming of the Lord, the distraction of which is put before us is horrific.

Look at what is happening today;

- Hurricanes
- Floods
- Storms
- Overflowing waters
- The eruption of volcanoes
- Mudslides
- Ground breakings
- The roaring of the heavens.

God is speaking to all of us, not just to a few. Many are losing families, family members, the main thing is children. You know, there use to be a saying and I think it still is, the young should burry the old, but yet, we have more of the old burying the young. There is so much to learn and to apply to faith and hope, because of the lives we have subjected in for the sake of God and how we are destroying ourselves in many ways of which we know nothing of.

Even though the Bible teaches the ancestry history of saints and leaders and all their experiences, there is still a picture painted for us to share in, in knowing the power of God's hand and His Glory of which He still today gives us, which is knowledge, and wisdom.

Proverbs teaches of the sword, the judgement, evil, not only that, also strength, and knowledge of how all of it is still apart of the world today. We as a people of many nationalities, and nations has to understand, there is no difference except for what we divided ourselves in knowing. Hebrew, Muslim, Japanese, Asian, African, Indian, Mexican, Black, White, Nigerian, it doesn't matter. There will always be a prejudice among us. We are still however, related in through the blood of Jesus.

The book of Ecclesiastes, God teaches us, everything has its time. What does that mean to us?

- Is it opening the minds to know this is a resting place and not our true home?
- Is it helping us to know we are not here forever?
- Is it throwing up a red flag to those who cannot comprehend the ending of time?
- Is it helping us to understand this is God's way of explaining His power over us?
- Do we understand the meaning of life and death?
- Do we take for granted the wonders of life?
- Do we take for granted the wonders of death?

There is so much we still have to learn. God's plan does not intel, you are the creator, you are in charge of anything without his authority over it. In other words, prayer and faithfulness in what He allows in your lives, is a significant part of why things happen for you. Yes, there are so many ways to twist the truth, until there is no understanding of how things truly come to pass. Everything has its time. The valuable intake of wisdom, honor, obeying authority, and understanding the end. Seeking God and revealing Him in your life, is a powerful statement of truth. Abide in Him and He in you, He will be the rock and the salvation of your success. Believing in God is a positive and most desirable inspiration of all times.

Song of Solomon, a beautiful beloved story of which we can share in our lives and in the desires of our minds. Yes, it has its design of faith, the design of pain and it shares how the respect of others, should be a factor in all life challenges, and knowing the depths of which it can obtain the love. The story takes in sight of how love can be painful and yet desirable. Not only in lives, but in countries and how we desire by touring other countries, of which we do, and we return with the inspiration to our own to share beauty of which is seen and not heard of. The story can be complicated, however, if reading and envisioning your thoughts on what is written, you can imagine the beauty of the connection in nations and nationalities, as well as in your own relationships of which you desire.

The book of Isiah a historical scene of wickedness, judgement, condemnation and the renewal. In this great story on Isaiah, he was called to be a prophet. God used Isaiah to share the stories of which we have read over and over again. Each time Isaiah is studied, the stories are revealing as he sees things which no man has seen, only he can witness the truth and the things God put before him, as he takes interest in sharing what was in those days. There was great power of God and His creation. God's powerful force and how He is the ruler of all things, should be a known factor of how we should know He is the Great I Am. The Lord showed much of His greatness in Isaiah, of how He shared is majestic glory. His command to Isaiah and the depth of His powers came known throughout the nations of who He is. The powerful hand of God is revealed many times and ways, because of the rebellion and the denying of people. The denial of trusting in God and what He can do, He still keeps us though as He did in the days of Isaiah.

The reasons of sharing these books designed to individually be carefully consumed with truth, the book of Isaiah, which God is revealing much of what is of his creative power, the demands were demanded by His hand. Through the book of Isaiah not speaking on each chapter, however, my trying to help you understand God is powerful in every way, and can be the force of every hand. In the book of Isaiah, God always presented himself through each design of vision.

Through Jacob, Moab, the vision of the valley, the proclamation of Tyre and other parts of the countries and what these places had to endure. What we as a people need to know is, God never leaves us, He gets angry with us and make changes. When we are weak, His strength out of nowhere comes in and takes over. He showed his hand to many parts of the book for the people to know who He is.

God sees everything in our lives, not just some, but everything. How many know about the salvation, the teachings, the wisdom, the sacrifices of which we live daily. God has always been the corner stone, and always will be. There are consequences which we as a people place upon ourselves, even though we feel we are in secret of it, however we are not, because there is a God, who sees your every hand. His words, "They shall know I Am the Lord God." He is not only speaking to one, He speaks to everyone. Nations, and nations.

The intercessions and the forsaken of our God have a powerful foundation, which we need to notice as we study and understand what God did then, He is able to do now. God remembers our transgressions and iniquities, He can bring down on us His fury, also His anger, yet He will never leave us or forsake us. He is our universe of which we live and breathe.

Jerimiah the son of Hilkiah, the prophet of whom God chose, was the watchmen, while he went through the command of God. Jeremiah endured much while being used by God. You constantly learn the hand of God and how inspiring it is to reveal how He is the God of gods, king of kings, Lord of lords. Jeremiah, as he went through his life, didn't want the duties put before him, because he was young and felt what God needed him to do was not on his level of presenting anything. However, God used Jeremiah even though he was imprisoned, because of what was told to him by God himself. God and His most inspiring way of touching those He chooses to put before us. Jeremiah was a great example of sharing the word and the life experience of who God was to him. He was told to write letters, speak them to the people, unfortunately they refuse to hear or acknowledge God.

It is an amazing journey of knowing what Jeremiah endured. Imprisonment of what was commanded by God, also was continually watched over by God. In the story of Jeremiah, which I will not reveal, what happen to Jeremiah and how his life was, because by reading and experiencing the most inspirational concept of this book, tells of how the power, once again, is inspirational, creative, revealing, invigorating, devotional, astounding, sorrowful, but yet desiring to know. The life of which we live today, we at some point take advantage of believing we are doing all this ourselves. Unfortunately, there is a limit of what you as a person can do. Without God there is no vision, without His vision, you have none, without His wisdom there would be none also.

There was destruction, false teachings, mourning of the prophet, even of the people. Jeremiah even questioned God, he got answers also from the Lord. God uses us as he did all the saints, just not the same way. Yes, we are stewardships of his word. We have leaderships of teachings through many types of beliefs. The words God used through Jeremiah was not believed in by his own people, therefore the accusations of false teachings were in those days also, and the punishment was prison, therefore Jeremiah's life was not as fortunate, but yet God held on to him through Grace and Mercy. You all know the saying,

- For God so love the world…….

In the book of Jeremiah there were many sights of which was known by God,

- Pride
- Backsliding
- Shame
- Sin
- Punishment
- Judgement
- Restoration

The revealing of much of which people do from generation to generation, should be a factor revealed of knowing, we have to constantly place ourselves in a position of needing God to be acknowledged. We as a people for many generations pass, have rebelled, reproached, reproved, fell down and fault others, and sometimes God for our own misunderstandings. We think our lives are our own, its not. Many may think their invincible, can continue to be in-exposable. Here in the book of Jeremiah you find, God sees and knows everything. Also, in the book you will learn of God's assurance through all He sees through the people. The journey not only speaks of Jeremiah.

It also speaks of great kings, such as;

- Nebuchadnezzar
- Zedekiah
- Baruch
- Micaiah
- Jehoiakim

Here was still much talk of Pharaoh and his army, the Chaldeans who besieged Jerusalem. The main concept is learning the hand of God, which we will never really know, because He says, "No man shall know my hand."

The book of Lamentation and the affliction of Jerusalem, also how God's anger was of Jerusalem.

- Why was God so angry with Jerusalem?
- Was He angry because of rebelliousness?
- Did He have reason to destroy them?

What we reveal is the wrath of God. God in this day will always be, yet, He will stand back and watch, as we know He is the master of every life. He covets us and He is also the restoring faith in us. We believe in God and what He can do. He continually waits on us, because of our own turns and decisions to leave him out of equations, even though He is always present.

The book of Ezekiel and the revealing of the beast. What is the beast in the life of many of us, is it known by man? How is it, the revealing of the Lord through the son of man is so defined, as in the chosen one Ezekiel. The Lord continued to speak to him and share the spirit of himself through Ezekiel. God was truly aware of the rebelliousness of Israel, wherefore the hand of God was shown many times, as did the continuing story of Pharaoh and his army. God made the son of man the watchman unto Israel, to warn the people. As in this life of which we live, God uses some one or all to reveal his presence, even though we know not his hand. Throughout the readings of these books, God's preparation for his son has not yet been revealed, because of all the rebellion and the abominations, transgressions, and iniquities of which had been throughout the walk of the nations. God's vision which has always been is to his Son. The way the journey of the old testament has been revealed, continued through the chosen leaders of which was and still is used by the word of God.

- ➢ Leaders of churches,
- ➢ leaders of politics,
- ➢ leaders of families,
- ➢ Of organizations, and of nations,

All of which we have through man, combined thoughts and creations of society.

Learning the wrath of God, and knowing the jealousy of Him, is the source of His power, vision, molding, creating, the using of his people, sharing His compassion, His love, His revelation of hope in us. God as I continue to say, see all of what we do, where we go, how we are in our daily walk. We all continue the falling short in everyday life, knowing we chose to do what is right or wrong. We continue to make choices, even though we are aware of what is seen by God.

The son of man is used by God in the continuing vision of what God has for the tomorrows of which we are not promised. The judgements of God on us as his people, has been an on-going test of trials and tribulation knowing He is the great I Am. The use of Ezekiel, and the word of the Lord, and how He spoke to him, he continued to reveal what He as God is preparing to do. Ezekiel was one of the prophets who seen and heard the vision of God as did others. He let him know what he was going to do because of the idolatry of Israel, even the judgement also of Israel, also the abominations in the temple which held destruction, therefore the revealing of His word was to let Ezekiel know, how He was going to use him in the times of which was needed for the judgement on his people for what all they were doing.

Life today is so intertwined with itself, to where if you look around there is cities on top of cities, nations on top of nations, wars on top of wars, rebellion, sin, mischief, iniquities, wickedness, and the list can go on.

- How do we define the word of God to our own visions?
- How do we stop being in control of what is not ours?

These are just questions of which we can began to understand, we are not in charge of anything. Yes, there are leadership of many levels of life. God's hand no man will know is a true statement of which He has revealed throughout the old testament. The word of God is the mighty force of which we need in our lies. Even in the days of old, Jerusalem, Judah, Israel, all were cities of which God built and tore down to show His power, His compassion and His anger.

- ➢ He is here today,
- ➢ He is real today,
- ➢ He is the mighty God today.

As history unfolds, our hand changes because of what is of greed in some fashion, God hand never changes. He sees all things and know what the tomorrows will bring, not us. We can continue to plan for future commitments, however, not all the time they will come about.

Through the trial and error, God still love Jerusalem even though the rebellion and the deceit was there, He still gave love to them as to others. God still find ways to show you, He is still in charge of your life, no matter what you go through, He is the strong hold of your life. We should never lean to our own understanding, because He allows things to happen for reason.

He knows of the things we do,

- Sin
- Transgression
- Iniquities

God knows our ways, our doings, He knows every corner of our being. He has the ultimate key which can open and close at any time.

Daniel, the interpreter, there was no one found like him. The magicians who came before the king Nebuchadnezzar who dreamed dreams, was troubled. As we know the story, none could share their thoughts of how the dreams affected the king. The magicians, astrologers, even the sorcerers, even the Chaldeans couldn't interpret the dreams. Therefore, Daniel was told to come forth. When there are things in your life which comes about, which you cannot control, who do you say can intercede to be able to help you understand what is happening. In the story, Daniel was called because God used him. The king Nebuchadnezzar wanted to kill the companions of Daniel, because they could not give the answer of the dreams, wherefore Daniel was soughed out because of Arioch the captain of the kings guard. Daniel explains to the king the dreams; However, we know God reveals the dream through Daniel the prophet. The story continued with the king falling to his face after Daniel reveals to him his dreams and he worshipped Daniel. He also offered oblation and sweet odors unto him.

There were three companions of Daniel;

- Shadrach
- Meshach
- Abednego

They were set over the affairs of the province of Babylon, wherefore Daniel sat in the gate of the king. The story of the fiery furnace of which we all know of how the three men was told they were going to die, however, God steps in, there was no burning of them, they came out as they were, fully clothe, not a cinch of burn. They trust God through their trial time, he delivered them. God can and will deliver you from any and all things, if you just give all to him. We as a society tries to step away from the main ingredient of our lives, to do what we think is right. Destroying one another with greed, selfishness, jealousy, adultery, deceit, control, and all we try to do ourselves, falls apart because of the refusing of God. Not all of us but I would say the majority of us, because God's kingdom is of few. Why do I say this? Because He gave to us multitude, nations of nations, generations of generation. He only has a few. Those are the few of which He uses to share his word. He gave us the world, and his only begotten Son. He gave us five senses, sight to see, mouth to speak, hands to touch, feet to walk, ears to hear.

- What do we see?
- What do we say?
- How do we feel?
- Where do we walk?
- What do we hear?

Are we using what God gave to us in the manner of His commandments, His statutes, His glory, His wonders, His graciousness, His salvation?

In the story of Daniel, God shows us his hand, not much of it, however, He reveals the wonders of His, majestic signs. The story says to us, He came forth in the midst of the fire, and saved Shadrach, Meshach and Abednego. Everyone, governors, captains, counselors all gathered, they say the miracle hand of God. The concept of knowing and needing God in our lives, is to understand there is nothing to hard for Him. He can and will do what he says, He will deliver you from all things, if you just believe in him. The book of Daniel is an awesome study of which we all should understand, God knows your sleepless nights, your troubled minds, your hidden agendas, also your weakest hours. When you continue to read, Daniel is in the lion's den, with the lions, vicious, hungry, ready for the meal of their lives. The reason of Daniel being placed there, was because of praying to God, your father. They found him praying to his God, our God. There was a concern from others, Daniel was rebelling against the rules of which was placed by Nebuchadnezzar. Therefore, as the story tells us Daniel was thrown in with the lions. He continued to have faith of course, because he served a living God. As we know, God sent his angel to shut the lions up, for they did not hurt Daniel. God's hand of glory and compassion, can work for us, if we just stand still and know He is God. His powerful force can be the force of which we can all be coveted with. God is an awesome God, who reign from heaven, He is the mighty one who can save you from yourselves, and still watch you make mistake after mistake after mistake. He did say, you will fall before me even through your iniquities, transgressions, and all your faults. Later on in the story Daniel saw the vision, even though others did not see, when he heard the voice of God's words, he went into a deep sleep on his face, there was a hand which the story tells us touched him, it set him upon his knees also upon on the palm of his hands. God has a way of revealing himself to us, even when we feel there is no way, there is a way. There is always a revealing force around us, if we just move out of the way and let God do what He has always done, take care of what is His, which is the whole world. You, me, fowls of the air, creatures of the earth, the land and everything in it.

It is His, yes, He has set us up with much, we as society has grown, the passion of God still lives. The world has changed and will continue to change, we just need to know who is in charge.

Hosea who was told by God, to take a wife of whoredoms also children of whoredoms. He did what was told of him by God. Here God is using another chosen one, to do his will not his own. understanding the concept of why God does the things He do, is to understand the story of which He tells through the prophets of faith. Hosea did what was told. God showed him the increase and multitude of his life.

There was Gomer whom he took from Diblaim, wherefore, there he conceived a son, Jezreel, which he later avenged upon the house of Jehu. Here God is using Hosea to send a message of knowing who He is. Even though we read the word of God, we sometimes do not embrace the words to understand the vision of God. God's vision with Hosea was to bring attention to His power of giving and taking away, God caused much to happen, because of the deceitful ways of whoredom, and the excessiveness of the unfaithful people.

There was the;

- House of Jezreel
- House of Israel
- House of Judah, which the Lord saved, not by bow or sword nor by battle, by horses nor by horsemen.

The daughter who was conceived, Loruhamah bared a son, whose name was Loammi, whom was not recognized by God. He refused them, wherefore the number of children of Israel was as the sand of the sea, and cannot be measured nor numbered.

God's vision of what conspired was to show us how this world today is no different than the world of which was in those days, we still have multitudes of sins among us, we still feel as though it is ok for the deceit, secrets, deceptions, abominations, steeling, murdering, and other shameful acts which God sees. God see everything and He allows things to happen for reason. This world is prepared for the Son of God. God's vision for the world is to always prepare it for His son.

As you see for centuries, life changes and challenges are of the hand of God. Yes, we make our decisions, and we also forget where and how our thoughts create and build throughout the journey. Many life generations from the time of beginning, when the world was created, it was all given through the hand of God. In the book of Hosea, even though the deceitful and whoredom was allowed, God still stood in knowing Israel was gong to return. God's plan for us not only come from good, it also comes from the bad. God's plan is to continue to know your tomorrows, which you know nothing of, because it is not set up for you to experience beforehand. God continues to love Israel in spite of their shameful ways.

There was the;

- Apostasy of Israel
- The judgement of Israel

The shame of Israel stood out before God, even though He loved them, they still sinned. In God's eyes, we as a people sins every moment. The things we do, the thoughts we have, the visions in sight. When studying the word of God, as you learn of the prophets and all the chosen ones, who were chosen to by God, there was a journey of which we experienced by not only the readers and authors, but the individuals who were intertwined with the word, which God commanded those who He used to bring the word to the world. Yes, God is a jealous God, even though He is, He is also a compassionate and forgiving God.

God is the Holy One of heaven and earth as we continue the journey. This is the most fascinating story which has been told time and time again. The old testament teaches us the vision of which God is still preparing every moment, every day, every week, every month, also every year in our human life, which He created all in a day. In the beginning God created not only the world, He also created you or me, He also saw there was darkness and then He gave light, you know the story. Reading and learning the inner and outer realm of what God's vision is, has inspired me to write, not change, but create a library of the individual books, so if there is a story of the Bible you choose to take the time to study you can.

This I hope can encourage you to use your Bible as a daily word of hope, passion, endurance, vision, preparation to begin a journey with God. In the book of Hosea was restored back to God, from the iniquity. This same should be for the people of the world, because of the iniquity,

- The transgressions,
- The idolatry,
- The faultlessness,
- The sorrows,
- The backsliding,
- The sins,
- The deceit,

This world today is no different than the worlds of yesterday. They were naive, illiterate, bashful, no understanding, weak, impartial, they had greed, jealousy, hatred, sorrow, all of which we live today. Israel being God's people rebelled, cursed, rejected, held to anger, they were a people who did backslide, had iniquity, sin, transgressed and still was forgiven, as we are forgiven each day.

The book of Joel, as God's spirit was shown to Joel in how and what He was to do in the land. He spoke to Joel telling him to speak to his children and they speak to their children, generations to generations. He went on to talk about the insects which were;

- Palmerworm
- Locust
- Cankerworm
- Caterpillar

These types of insects, were without number, they were strong and were able to destroy. We have yet to see the change of which will come to the earth, which we call home. Is there an understanding of the fig tree, the pomegranate tree, the palm tree, the apple tree even the trees of the field? We still see them today in this world we live in. There is something about the trees, which we do not pay close attention to. In the days of the old testament, in Joel they withered, because the joy had left. During this time the Lord shows his hand. Everything was destroyed by fire, by the drying of the rivers, also the rotting of the seed. The same is happening today, even though we still feel we are here forever, which we are not. God has always throughout the stories, shared with us His mighty power, through the good and the bad. He continues to let us know, He will never leave us in spite of our faults, and never forsake us in spite of our doings, because He is a Mighty God who shows compassion, comfort, assurance and his hand of Grace and Mercy. When we do see the day of the Lord, we will experience his power;

- His forceful strength,
- His anger,
- His wisdom
- His judgements and all of which we have yet to acknowledge.

Everyday, there is signs of His presence, which some chooses not to see, hear or feel. In the book of Joel, the Lord reveals his hand with a

- day of darkness,
- day of gloom,
- day of clouds also of thick darkness

The experience of these things of which we have not, will also come to pass in the seasons of which God will put before us, as He did in the days of old. We are not exempted from what will be, the world belongs to the great and powerful, and most Majestic being. The universe is His and His alone. We should not lose sight of who is in charge and Who is above all. Yes, He gave to us many things which we can use to build and to expand, yet, we sometimes feel He is not needed. I am here to say; He is always needed in spite of anything we do and say. God in Joel, judges the nations, all nations not one or two.

When He brought again the captivity of Judah and Jerusalem, He also brought them into the valley of Jehoshaphat. The story always has a point of which God is saying there is nothing you can do or say that He has not heard or seen. When God judges the world for its transgression and iniquities, the hope in using the word of God to understand His vision, should be a solution to why He do what He do. God is the Mighty and Powerful Ruler over all the earth. He is the creator of the earth. everything we build shall come down on the day of his coming.

It is happening already;

- ➢ When storms pass through,
- ➢ Volcanoes erupt,
- ➢ Hurricanes come over the land,
- ➢ Earth quakes break the ground,
- ➢ Tsunamis overflows the land,
- ➢ Wars of wars which will never stop, continues to take one another.

We should all know, when the day of the Lord shows his hand, which no man will never know, the earth will shake, cry and moan. There will be change, not by us, however it shall come by the hand of God. Reading and listening to the word of God, helps you to know Him and understand His wonders, which we live throughout life challenges. These stories are so inspiring, it gives great expectations of how we are to have a need inside of us to have the desire to explore and experience the signs and wonders of our Lord, for He is the Magician of the word. It is the story of all stories, truth of all truth, which has been retold in every language, every nation, every generation, for the Lord God says, you will know me, "I Am He."

In the book of Amos, God showed His strength once again with the judgement of Judah and Israel. He punished Israel and their families for their iniquities. God's design in the old testament throughout the journey, reveals who He is in many segments of life, as change and challenges come about for his people and for the people he chose. He also let them know what he was going to do, as he did in Amos, He described what was going to happen and how He will use his word to create a vision to the people. The revealing of His secret unto His prophets was through the roaring of the lion, the blowing of a trumpet, also an adversary shall be round about the land. God showed his strength, by drying up the waters, He also struck the trees and gardens, wherefore the palmerworm killed them all. God has continued to show His people how he overthrown as He did with Sodom and Gomorrah.

When God sees, you are not hearing nor listening to Him, He has a way of opening your eyes. Look at what is happening today. Everyone see the problem at hand, yet there is no one on earth that can change the situation. God put things in place for reason. The reason is for you to know He is God. In the book of Amos, Israel has fallen, Gilgal went into captivity, for the word of the Lord was told to them to seek him.

He who made the seven stars:

- ➢ Turned the shadows of death into the morning,
- ➢ Make the day dark with night,
- ➢ Who also called the waters of the sea,
- ➢ Even poured them upon the face of the earth.

Who would you say is more powerful than God to do this? No one. This world and everything in it are for the Lord. The reading of his word is to help you to understand, we own nothing.

Yes, the industry of building

- Communities,
- Businesses,
- Possessing lands,
- Creating images,

How would you identify yourselves with what you read, when God has revealed everything to you? When God says to you in many ways, I know your transgression, your iniquities, your mighty sins. In the book of Amos, the signs are there of what you should do, you should seek;

- Good and not evil
- Hate the evil and love the good

God's hand in your life is to survive you from the depth of what comes when you as a people refuse to understand His way of commitment from you, the ten commandments, the statutes, also His remembrance of which He put before you. God gives everything to us, and for many centuries, decades of life He as open doors of which can or cannot be closed by man, only He has the ability. When he closes them, do we understand, why? In the end Israel was restored, do we understand why?

God's plan and preparation throughout the Old Testament, is showing who He really is, and amazing force of;

- Salvation,
- Righteousness,
- Truth, and
- Protection.

We ask for the Armor to be placed upon us daily, because of our own faults, not because of anyone else. We as a people keep wanting to find ourselves. If we just call on God, the Father, the Son and the Holy Spirit, He can and will help you. He is a mighty God whom we serve.

The book of Obadiah, where the Lord is speaking concerning the heathen and all of which is of the prophecy of Edom. Here the Lord is revealing how Obadiah has been made small among the heathen, He even showed him the pride of which was in his heart. When God can reveal your pride, what more can He reveal in your weakness, for you to understand who He is. There were thieves, robbers, and grapegathers, who were described in Obadiah. The question to Esau was how are the things of Esau searched.

The deception and prevailing of them who also ate the bread of Obadiah, also wounded him. In this short passage the Lord is near and is revealing to Obadiah his hand of which He is telling the heathen, as you have done, it shall be done unto you, for your reward shall retuned upon your own head. When deceit and deception is before you, you will experience the void in your life, also you will lose yourself because of your wrong doings. God sees everything and He knows all your doings according to your works. Nothing you do in this life or the next, God does not know.

Through every walk of life God speaks.

➢ The revealing of restoring faith, the deliverance, and holiness.

God speaks of possession and captivity, and when he comes the kingdom will always be acknowledged as His. We often find ourselves exposing ourselves, because we feel we own things. however, as God watches everything, His way of showing you He is of all power, He breaks down and build, for He wants you to know He is the Great I Am.

In the book of Jonah, the word came to Jonah to go to a place called Nineveh, a great city. However, we know he ran to another place called Tarshish trying to hide himself from God. God cannot be ignored, even in this day. He allows things to happen. Jonah went to Joppa where he found a ship going to Tarshish, the story unfolds, because he is still trying to ignore the Lord. God sent out a great wind, a might tempest was in the sea. The ship where Jonah was hiding from the Lord, was likely to be broken. So, the captain of the ship came to Jonah and asked, "Call upon your God" In the story Jonah reveals he is a Hebrew. What happen to Jonah? Because Jonah feared God as he told the captain, wherefore they were afraid. When God come to you in some fashion, are you afraid, or you aware of his presence. There are things in your life that happens because God is in your presence.

He reveals through;

- Prayer
- Through spirit
- Through your thoughts
- Through family
- Through meditation
- Through sorrow
- Through weeping
- Through laughter

There are so many ways God comes to us, even when we are just doing nothing.

In the story God prepared something for Jonah, because he was thrown into the sea. a great fish which swallowed Jonah up. There are things God does for you without your knowledge, to help you, even though you would never understand why, because you will always feel you did it on your own.

Jonah prayed to the Lord, for his affliction. Jonah began to call out with a cry unto the Lord, the Lord as we know heard him. Therefore, the great fish vomit Jonah unto dry land. The Lord came to Jonah a second time, telling him to go to Nineveh the great city to preach, Jonah then did what the Lord told him to do.

When God speak do you listen or do you say;

- Next time, or
- I'm too busy,
- Not now Lord I'm in the middle of something
- I got this Lord

God already know your tomorrows, you have no clue what the tomorrows bring, because they are not promised. The revealing of the change in Jonah came from his anger, which Jonah spoke of to God, saying, why he fled to Tarshish. He knew God was a kind and gracious God, and a merciful God, slow to anger. He asked the Lord to take his life. However, God had something else instore for Jonah, he prepared a gourd, making it over Jonah for it would be a shadow over his head. God is a compassionate God, if you can see beyond yourself centered ways and trust Him. He will do his will and comfort you in any trial of your life. In the story, He gave a second chance, He can do the same for you. we know He forgives seventy times seven, in all walks of life and challenges of which we put ourselves in.

Deception is of ourselves. We are our worst enemy, even though we have the audacity to accuse others for our own misfortunes. We are our own worst enemies.

The book of Micah, there was Rulers and Prophets. In this story, the Lord appeared on the earth, He saw where there was iniquity, transgression, shame, also sin. There was violence and oppression. With all these things being experienced in the land, the people cried out to God, however He did not hear them. He also hid His face from them, because of their doings. As we know, we are not exempt from our doings of today. We are constantly challenging God indirectly as well as direct, because we have everything before us, as though we gave to ourselves. God is the powerful ruler over all things. In Micah, we find all of which has happened God still is God. He establishes in the mountains and exalt above the hills where people shall flow. When we feel we are in charge, we forget God is the master of all plans, yet we as a people feel we don't need Him. Not everyone is of denied fault, there are some who believe, there are some who don't believe.

We have many types of religions today of which some worship;

- Those who worship idols,
- Some worship spirits,
- Some just trust in God and know Him,
- Some are non-believers and some don't have a clue of who they are.

In the story of Micah, it speaks about how the son dishonors the father and the daughter rises up against the mother, the daughter in law against her mother in law, wherefore the man's enemies are the men of his own house.

Trust   Obedience   Honor   Respect   Loyalty   Love.

Backsliding   Disobedience   Dishonesty   Disrespect   Deceit   Hate.

This all happens in every home, somewhere, somehow. What causes these things to happen in our lives?

- ➢ Do we really know?
- ➢ Can we analyze the problems or solve the equations ourselves?

We should know that a house built on sand will sink, a house built on a stone will not sink. What structure do your house stand? Is God a strong hold in your lives, is He the God of Mercy and Truth. We all will go through trying times such as trials, failures, deceit, backslidings, shame, sorrow, and anger. Life challenges do not stop. God is aware of everything that passes through your lives. He is the God of all. God has compassion for all he will subdue our iniquities. God is the power of which we shall seek, for he can help you through all things.

The book of Habakkuk, the burden of which he was under, how long did he cry to the Lord? In grief, and violence, strife and contention, there was judgement. The wicked which deals treacherously and devours him who is more righteous. In wickedness all these acts of which Habakkuk cried out, were believed to have been a troublesome worry, wherefore he cried out to the Lord to reprove him. When we are in trouble or, should I say when the enemy has entered your lives, and is there to destroy you because they find your weakness, there is a possibility, you will not know when and why it happen.

The question will be;

- ➢ why!

- ➢ What!
- ➢ How did it happen!
- ➢ Where did it come from!
- ➢ When did it start!

Well, it started when you made decision to not give everything to God. Many people or nations today is struggling trying to understand the wicked things happening in their lives or their world. Look at the world today, wickedness, deceit, destruction, invasion, violence, bitterness, greed, and the list continue.

Look at the schools, churches, politics;

- ➢ God has been removed, prayer has been removed, violence, guns as protection has been placed before Him who rules, no strong security,
- ➢ God is not being recognized, burning of the faithful home of where God should be strong and mighty, thieves break in and steal,
- ➢ Government has no control, trust has been laid to the side, there is no foundation of belief, God has not been recognized, greed, violence, abstinence, failure of trust, fear of power, weakening of strength in knowledge.

There has been much change, for God knows there is a time of which He will show His hand, when you lease expect.

The Lord answered Habakkuk with these words, "Write the vision, make it plain upon tables, for he who reads it may run."

The words that was written, was for an appointed time, yet at the end, it shall speak it will not tarry. Even though his soul is lifted the just shall live by faith. When you trust in God's word and your faith is in Him who rules, you will know the power of God is stronger than any thing you face.

When God speaks, He tells you through many designs of vision;

- Through spirit and truth
- Through the storms and hurricanes,
- From the depth of the sea,
- From the mountains of volcanoes which cries out,
- From the earthquakes and tsunamis,

God speaks from heavens and earth, because he knows how to get your attention. When change began in our lives from nations to nation, generations to generation, there became a passing void where some has forgotten. We as a people change, God does not change. He stands back and let you fall, yet He never leave you or forsake you. Why is that?

When the word says "Woe to the Wicked"

- What does this mean in your life?
- How can you fix your situations or circumstances on your own?
- When did you decide to give up on God?
- What happen when you did?

The prayer of Habakkuk to God was, he as the Lord to revive His word in the midst of the years, even in wrath remember Mercy. God came and glory covered the heavens and earth, through everything God was an everlasting force. As he is in our lives. When all fails, He is still our God. The power which has miraculous strength comes from God, how is it many say, He does not exist, when everything and everyone, He designed and made whole.

- God is a jealous God,
- He is a compassionate God,
- He is an angry God,
- He is a Mighty God,
- He is a Merciful God,
- He is silent.

If he can bring down the troubled walls of life, what is it he cannot do in your troubled times. God does work in season, because He has given four to the world of which we live, summer, spring, winter and fall, whereas they use to be of a season, now they are together as one season, if you get the irony of it. Life does not start or stop with you being in charge, it stops and starts when God hand has been shown, through anger or compassion. When the saying of "God's unchanging hands" has been spoken, He has never left, He watches you daily through His eyes and your inner minds. Meaning, your soul, your vision, your thoughts, your faith, your deceit, your wrong doings, your right doings, everything according to your doings and your unawareness of yourselves. He knew you before you were conceived, and your destiny of where you will end up.

The prayer ends with Habakkuk "The Lord God is my strength, He will make my feet like hinds' feet, he will make me walk upon mine high places." When you pray what is your faith and how strong is your fear in God. He is the powerful one who can see all things. you can hide, yet you are never hidden.

The book of Zephaniah, the judgement and sacrifices, punishments and the wrath of God. The Lord's vision was with great design. When He came unto Zephaniah, He came with great demand of what He was going to do as judgement on the nations. He consumes that of which He gave of the land through out the nations of the world. He consumed man and beast. The word of God has spoken so many times and ways, He still do it today, through many ways of which we will never be able to find answers for. He explains His doings to Zephaniah.

His words;

- I will consume all things from off the land,
- I will consume man and beast
- I will consume the fowls of the heaven, the fishes of the sea
- I will consume the stumbling blocks with the wicked
- I will cut off man from the land.

Can you comprehend the word of God and the wrath of his hand when you are put in judgement for your doings?

He goes on to say;

- I will stretch out mine hand upon Judah also upon Jerusalem
- I will cut off the remnant of Baal also the Chemarims with the priest.

God continue to use Zephaniah as his speaker to try and get the attention of those who turned away. Many of us turn away from God, to say we can make our own decisions. Parents and children, as we grow from infants to teens, we graduate in to adulthood, not understanding the realism of what it is to achieve, or progress in faith. We assume before we are convinced, we are God's children and the scale of life is what He designed for us and through us.

God's way of embracing us is not to award you, but to receive your faith so you can know Him. How do we get through our daily activities of life, or our maturity of growth without going through the pains of which was designed? Everything in life today was already designed through the hand of God. In Zephaniah God speaks, His determination of gathering nations together because of the wickedness, the filth and polluted cities of which did not conceived the correction. When you do not hear the word of the Lord for correction, you will be destroyed. The jealousy of God is when you part from him and worship other gods, or idols, or take part in greed, selfishness, and not believing He is the God of all creations. All you have and has received and accomplished or failed, is not from you. all things of this earth are God's, all things built by man will perish. All things of the world belong to God. Generations to generation, nations to nations, there has been elevation, cities have grown, nations have overflow with power, multitudes of life have been a favor, the increase of life has been awesome in growth. How do you not see the hand of God? He has always been the factor of everything and everyone. The tools He put before man began in the beginning of time;

- ➢ Land with wilderness of trees

- Mountains and hills
- Valleys and rivers of water
- Forests of blooms of beauty

These things which was given by God, has been from the beginning of time. The cities of which is spoken of throughout the word of God, to name a few;

- Jerusalem
- Judah
- Israel
- Egypt
- Babylon

A few of many we now know. God own you and everything you have and accomplished in your lifetime. When you take God out of the equation of your life, failure began to gradually take over. Look around and through the eye of your neighbors. There is much to be said about what is happening today. We are God's people, and what happen in the old testament is happening now. God is hear, awaiting to know what your plan is, because His plan is far better and stronger, and connects more than anything you have to study to put together. As for God, His plan is already in place. He knew you before you were born, He knew you was a mix up, a mess up and a sinner in your own right. Truth be told, you did not know who you were until you were able to understand your father and mother, whom was chosen to raise you, nurture you, teach you, adore you, bring you up and make ready your journey of which God knew before you knew. Yes, there are many broken families, rejected families, so on and so forth, which has not given its all and all. Families of destruction because of the selfishness, and greed.

Obeying the hand of God, trusting in Him, knowing everyone will have to fall at his feet, asking for forgiveness, asking for restoration, asking for the touch of the hem of the Garment, also to cry the tears of pain and suffering. What god can you rely on to favor you through everything. The wickedness in Zephaniah, God showed his hand, letting them know everything will be taken and destroyed, because they did not hear Him. God is a jealous God, who will destroy your path, if you do not hear.

The book of Haggai, once again God spoke to Haggai the prophet. In speaking to him, he says "Consider your ways" There was a passage which the Lord revealed to Haggai'

- You have sown much, yet brought in little,
- You eat, yet you have not enough,
- You drink, yet you are not filled with drink,
- You are clothed, yet there is none warm,
- He who earn wages earn wages to put it into a bag with holes.

These passages of which is spoken by God to Haggai, has meaning. In comparison to our lives, the industry of life has overbearingly consumed so much, in land houses, businesses, social media, automobiles, also financial gain. The appetite of society has taken in so much, until it is overbearingly full and has elevated itself until it is not being satisfied. It has also consumed itself with desires of more and more until the cup of life is not fulfilling. The shelter of protection has grown so much, until it is not recognized because of greed. The industry has grown and build infrastructures of financial gain, until now there is so much the deceased are being removed from their proper place, so society can build more and more.

There is so much equity in society today, that it has an emptiness which will not be revealed until Jesus come and show them the treacheries and the corruption of which society fills with greed, zeal, violence, darkness, division also judgement. We as a society in some fashion do not hear, nor see, nor share in understanding why the world is and who is in charge, the way of the world is the way of the world. God hand of power will reveal His way according to our doings.

The book of Zechariah, the displeasing of the Lord God. God uses Zechariah to speak to the people of their ways and doing, which He tries to command them to turn from, which they did rebel with evil doings. Even though we as God's people have increased in many ways and fashions of life, there is still many who don't believe God is real. God sees and knows as I will continue to say, everything, every move, every secret you hold. He will judge you according to your doings. As he mentioned to Zechariah, son of Berechiah;

> ➢ I saw by night, behold a man riding a white horse, he stood among the myrtle trees which were in the bottom, also behind him were red horses, speckled and white. Therefore, the question was asked, "What are these?

There was an angel who spoke to Zechariah explaining to him the meaning. They were sent to and fro through the earth.

Today can you say the angels are among us? Can you say they watches over us even through our darkest hour, our deepest thoughts, our storms of humility? Through the book of Zechariah, the angel continued to show the way by answering the questions of the things that was seen through Zechariah. God uses us in his own way. He can and has shown us, we are just who we are. He has leaders and followers of whom we set before;

- On a Sunday morning,
- On the jobs,
- In our schools and colleges,
- Even in our homes, hospitals, even in funeral homes, and cemeteries.

There is always going to be authority through leaders of any type of vision. However, God is in control of all things, large and small. There was questioning of the lamp, by which the angel again spoke with Zechariah, he asks what was seen, Zechariah answered, he described it as;

- A candlestick all of gold
- Seven lamps
- Seven pipes to the seven lamps
- Two olive trees one on the left and one on the right of the bowl

Therefore, he asked what are these? The answered was by night, nor by power, but by my spirit. If life is so perfect, how would you feel if an angel would ask what do you see, when you look at the world through you own eyes? How would you vision this world? God already knows what you see, even how it displeases Him. There is so much society has built, for the knowing of Jesus and His coming is unpredictable, because of all of what is happening today. God allows things to happen in this life, because distraction is a huge factor of how we have built in many ways in this society. Abominations, violence, corruption, greed, zeal, judgement, division, death, rebellion, backsliding, adultery, swearing, and others, the list continues.

How will you face your failures, will you run, hide, cry, blame others, or will you fall and pray, plead for forgiveness, ask for God to order your steps? What is the message today? The world is in dying help of God to show a new creation of himself, even though we think this is our home. This is not our home; it is a place where we as a people reside until the coming of the Lord. Facing ourselves, and our doings, we will be held accountable according to what God has already seen and heard. We will worship the Lord God in a different way when He comes. We all has fallen short of the Glory of the Lord, now is the time for repentance and forgiveness. Yet, we continue to hold on to the things of the world, without facing the consequences of our own greed and self-control. God still rules.

The book of Malachi the burden of the Lord to Israel by Malachi. The passage verse found Malachi 3:6-8, is a passage which we all know and tries to respect. There are some who can and there are some who cannot. It says;

- For I am the Lord, I change not; Therefore, your sons of Jacob are not consumed.
- From the days of your fathers you are gone away from mine ordinances, you have also not kept them. Return unto me, for I will return unto you, you then said, "Wherein shall we return?"
- Will a man rob God? Yet you have robbed me. However, you say, "Wherein have we robbed you?"
- In tithes and offerings.

These words are spoken in every church through out the nation.

- What would you say tithes are recognized as?
- How much is enough?
- What would you say is enough?
- How do you give?

- What do you give?

The more you give the more you receive. Now some can only give themselves, some can't give anything, because they do not have. How is this measured. I'm not to insult anyone, however, this is a very serious issue, which is addressed to those who are able, unfortunately there are some who just don't have. The woman who gave just what she had, two pennies, she gave much in the sight of God. There is much to be said of tithing. Yes, we have the rich who has much more than anyone, yet they may just put what they feel they want, there are some who will give graciously. There is the not so rich but middle classed, who may not have as much, yet they give more than the rich, then there is those who are struggling to keep a roof over their heads and their family, who will give the 10% of which is asked. Then there are those who have nothing who come with prayer in their hearts, and asking God to accept them. who would you say is more acceptance in God's eye?

- The rich
- The middle class
- The struggling family
- The poor

God says, "Bring your tithes into the storehouse, for there may be meat in mine house, and prove me not, if I will open you the windows of heaven and pour you out a blessing, there shall not be room enough to receive it."

God is a powerful and understanding God, who do not turn away from any giving. He sees your heart, He knows your thoughts, He comforts your sorrows, He holds you through all sacrifices, He knows you. God accepts all offerings, large or small, even when there is none to give, He still accepts you for giving you. The Lord loves everyone, not just the rich, not just the middle class, not just the struggling families, not just the poor, all creations. God accepts us for who we are in Him, not for who we choose to become. You have to wonder;

- If you are rich, how did you get there, do you give much more than what you have received through the vision you built for you?
- If you are the middle class, do you give according to your earnings?
- If you are the struggling family, do you take from Peter to pay Paul in order to give?
- If you are poor, do you bring yourselves to Christ as you are?

When God says bring you tithes into the store house, is He saying, money, or is he saying yourselves. God's house is full of great things, He blesses you just for you giving him glory, honor, faith and trust, because you give to Him yourselves. Yes, tithes and offering for the buildings of this day and others, are to be able to continue to have the doors of the churches open for all believers as well as non-believers. The church is built of sinners, whoremongers, adulterers, thieves, haters, rich, poor, average, and others whom you can bring to mind. God turns away from those who do not hear or see, of have faith the size of a mustard seed. Those who rebel, commit abominations, choose to reject the statutes, chose to lean not to his understanding, choose not to commit to the commandments, choose not to hear Him. God's anger is brought upon the world because of rebelliousness, greed, selfishness, corruption, iniquity, and transgression.

Conclusion

Throughout the Old Testament, the inspiration of all has been a journey of realism and truth. Finding ways to please God and know who He is, He is the Mighty and Powerful God of all creations. The preparing of this world of which He constantly does from generation to generation, nations to nations, He is still the God of all gods.

As we go through the changes, challenges, creativity, industrial craft of this world, God still works. His whole vision is the preparation of this world for his Son. Remember you are a vessel; His Son stands above you. as we go through life thinking because we hold a position, we are above the one below us. We have no position; we earn a position. The Son of our God, the creator of everything, is the sole proprietor of everything. The journey of life was a gift which is given continually through the hand of God. His Son as he carried his own cross to Calvary was nailed, crowned, pierced, and raised up on that old rugged cross for all not just for some, but for all our lives.

Taking time to read and understand this world does not belong to you, we live and we die, life and death, is what we do. God gives to us daily, and believes we will give back to him through prayer, and faith of knowing and recognizing who He is. Understand the preparation of God's vision. Know His purpose, understand His comings, take heed to His commandments, and statutes. Repent and know every one who told the story lived the story. We now as a people, reads the story, but yet we change the story to meat our own understanding. God's word never changes, His word is sufficient, powerful and tell you a story of truth. Speculating and challenging His word is not the way. There are preachers and teachers, who can help you in understanding the word.

God himself is the only one who can reveal to you His truth. Have the faith the size of a mustard seed. Believe in God and know He is God.

Thank you for taking the time to trust and to know, God is who He is, the God of hosts, creator, leader, the majestic and powerful proprietor of the world. He can do all things.

Yvonne Porter Young

Copyright April 2019

www.ingramcontent.com/pod-product-compliance
Lightning Source LLC
Chambersburg PA
CBHW041526220426
43670CB00002B/41